5 Simple Skills to Crack the Nut on Relationships

Jennifer Byrnes

Illustrations by Lisa Fenton

Tasora

Tasora Books
5120 Cedar Lake Road
Minneapolis, MN 55416
(952) 345-4488
Distributed by Itasca Books
Printed in the U.S.A.

Cover design by Sue Jenkins and John Houlgate
Original cover art by Lisa Fenton
Original artwork for entire book by Lisa Fenton

Disclaimer: Any connection to any person living or deceased is purely coincidental; the names in these stories have been changed.

Library of Congress Cataloging-in-Publication Data

Byrnes, Jennifer

We're All Nuts: 5 Simple Skills to Crack the Nut on Relationships/ Jennifer Byrnes

Summary: Learn to connect in any situation with skills to help build your business or personal relationships.

Interpersonal Communication, Team-building, Relationships, Generational Differences, Technology Challenges to Communication

ISBN 978-1-934690-94-9

1. Business & Econ. – Non-Fiction   2. Self Help – Non-Fiction   3. Family & Relationships – Non-Fiction

Printed in the United States of America

To all of the extraordinary nuts in my life.

Contents

Appendix

A Message for You on Meaningful Connections in our Nutty World

Welcome to the Nut Party! Thank you for sharing your time with me and trusting there will be value in my message. With the bit of trust you already have, we're off to a good start building our nut-cracking relationship!

Have you ever done something nuts?

Have you thought someone was nuts (for something they did or said)?

Have you felt like you're going nuts?

Have you loved something so much you were nuts for it?

Have you adored someone so much you were nuts about them?

We're all nuts! And like actual nuts, we have an outer shell and kernel; our persona and inner self (inner nut). Meaningful connections are established when our shell is cracked and we share part of our inner nut. Over time, as we continue to share, a relationship forms.

Effective relationships are the key to success—igniting energy and possibility within us. Through the metaphors, research, and real-life stories in this book, I intend to reawaken people to the power of interpersonal communication to meaningfully connect, build trust, and form deeper, more effective relationships.

You'll notice that trust is mentioned frequently throughout the book to emphasize the leading role it plays in effective relationships. When I think about trust, there are qualities that I look for in others, and others look for in me. What else might you add?

Trust	
Authentic	Accountable
Honest	Appreciative
Loyal	Fair
Open	Respectful

I have dedicated my career to helping teams and individuals connect with others, and build the relationships that enable greater personal and professional success. *We're All Nuts* highlights the challenges we face building them (Part I), and shares how to make the connections needed to forge them (Part II).

May you live long, crack many nuts, and prosper!

Jennifer

Part I

Our Nutty World

Chapter One

The Importance of Real (Effective) Relationships

I was five years old and my family had just moved to a house in Bloomington, Minnesota. As a quiet, shy kid I had only one friend; a distant memory left behind, like the mounted deer head in the basement of our old house. To lessen my loneliness, I created an imaginary best friend, Shorla (that's right, "Shorela"), who played school, house, and restaurant with me. But I was still a lonesome nut and Shorla was not enough; I had to do everything and she was pretty boring. I wanted a real friend to build forts and with whom I might go on adventures.

One magical day, our new next-door neighbors, a family with a son and a daughter, stopped by to say "hello." The girl was a bit younger than I, but she was a real kid, and when she asked, "Do you want to play?" my face lit up and formed an ear-to-ear smile. I was overwhelmed with excitement. "Yes!!" I exclaimed.

Over the next several years, we built hundreds of forts and had countless adventures. We donned camo, tree branches, and flashlights, transforming ourselves into the neighborhood spies. We played school, house, and restaurant. We made dance videos, had sleepovers, watched movies, and rode our bikes to Tom Thumb for Snickers bars and New York Seltzer Vanilla Cream Sodas. Just being together made life fun and exciting! She was a real friend. I realized how important real relationships were in life, and I wanted more!

As children, we need real—not imaginary—relationships to build confidence and a sense of security, and to satisfy our need to play, grow, and have fun. As adults, we need real relationships to feel fulfilled, achieve our goals, and maximize our potential. Whether we are children or adults, real relationships feel trusting, positive, and mutually beneficial: they are effective. Success, personal and professional, is grounded in building and maintaining effective relationships.

The verbal and non-verbal information collected during in-teractions, especially face-to-face, feeds the interpersonal com-munication process, which creates a single social reality for the participants, forming their relationship.[1] We mentally process the information to interpret and understand how a person is in that moment (know the nut), and then adapt ourselves to complement the other person (like selecting the right nut-cracking tool) in order to strike common ground and make a connection—the nut is cracked! This processing ability is a facet of Emotional Intelligence (EQ), a theory introduced by Peter Salovey and John D. Mayer in 1990.[2] By intentionally using interpersonal communication and EQ, we interact with others in a mindful and meaningful way, enabling us to know the nut, crack it, and begin building an effective relationship.

Party Fun!

On Sunday, September 3, 2017 the first Nut Mixer experiment was launched. My husband and I invited many of our closest friends and family to share in the "We're All Nuts" endeavor. I secured thirteen varieties of raw nuts in their shells and asked all guests (ranging from eight to seventy-five years) to experience cracking and tasting them. They were asked to record their observations on look, feel, smell, sound, taste, and anything else that came to mind with each particular nut. No other instructions were given.

Good, Old-Fashioned Fun

Each guest was equipped with a pen, clipboard, beverage of choice (to get the creative juices flowing), and "Nutty Observations" worksheets, then set loose to get cracking. Everyone gathered around the dining room table, mingling, cracking nuts—shells flying everywhere—talking, laughing, and recording their nutty thoughts on the worksheets. Some guests knew each other, many did not (or not very well), but everyone interacted. Every guest was fully engaged and appeared to genuinely enjoy the activity.

Results

Some nuts were lovingly embraced, and others were vehemently rejected. There certainly were similarities between responses, but there were far more differences, and in some cases stark, polar-opposite opinions about the same nut. Let's take, for example, the Pili Nut. Most guests had never heard of this nut. Some adored it, declaring it was unique and *wonderful, while others hated it, describing it as unusual and gross.*

An unplanned and unexpected result of the experiment was that no one was on their smartphone, in some cases for a couple of hours! Since everyone had to manage a clipboard and pen while cracking nuts, tasting, and imbibing, they really couldn't physically manage a phone in hand. However, it was a heart-warming sight!

Since everyone shared a purpose to crack nuts, taste the nuts, and record their nutty thoughts, everyone had an immediate connection and enjoyed interacting with one another. Smartphones were not missed!

People are Nuts

No one is exactly the same as anyone else. This simple activity underscores the differences in perception; no one has exactly the same view as another person. Like the varied perceptions and opinions about the nuts, people read and interpret each other differently based on situation, environment, and experiences, which are continually changing. Our perception of someone may be completely different from someone else's, based on our unique interactions and changes that occur within our respective environments and experiences. Others' perceptions of us will vary based on the same factors. And everyone's thoughts may shift tomorrow—based, again, on ever-changing situations, environments, and experiences. Similarly, repeating the experiment at a later date with the same people will not yield exactly the same results; I tested this with a handful of willing nut lovers from the original

Nut Mixer. In short, building and maintaining effective relationships requires a constant awareness of ourselves and others to Know the Nut in order to appropriately adapt and crack it.

The other important take-away from this experiment is the importance of meaningful connections. Like cracking a nut to get to the kernel (inner nut), people need authentic connection points to get to know each other (inner self), and to begin building an effective relationship. How can you become an expert nut-cracker? First, let's take a look at the modern-day challenges.

Check It Out!

You can find the different nut profiles (shell/persona and kernel/inner self attributes) based on the responses from the Nut Mixer in the Appendix. Take a look and ponder the following questions:

- ❖ *Do you know any "nuts" who fit the nutty descriptions provided by my guests?*

- ❖ *How adept are you at adapting yourself to crack different "nuts"?*

- ❖ *What kind of "nut" might you be … today?*

Chapter Two

Modern-Day Challenges

John was an outstanding engineer who worked on an emerging technology and his work was extremely complicated. He was so good at what he did that he was responsible for one of the largest and most lucrative deployment regions for the company. The problem was that many people outside of the team thought he was rude and grumpy, so they refused to contact him directly. This burdened his teammates and manager, but also didn't sound like the guy his boss knew; John was quiet and kept to himself, but got along well with his peers, and was very nice and accommodating when his manager needed something from him.

His boss had a hunch about the problem; virtually all of John's communication with people outside of the team was conducted through email. And although John was always responsive and concise in his replies, every word, even to his boss, was CAPITALIZED. John may not have realized that the use of caps conveys SHOUTING! John's manager discussed his observation with him. John responded with shock and genuine embarrassment. He explained that he always kept the Caps Lock key on for consistency (because he worked with command line interfaces all day long). John's new awareness allowed him to make a simple change that resolved a very big, unintended problem!

John's story highlights the important role of interpersonal communication in connecting with others. If either John or his offended colleagues had met in person, or even picked up the phone to talk instead of email, they probably would have had very different—

and likely positive—interactions. His colleagues would have realized John wasn't rude or grumpy, but was actually eager to help. Instead of avoiding John, they'd get to know him, and probably build an effective relationship.

The many different corporate roles I've held had several things in common: 1) highly technical teams, 2) diversity among the nuts (gender, culture, race, experience, education, etc.), and 3) driving change to improve efficiency, productivity, and/or quality. Regardless of the nut assortment, in every case, every time, applying the 5 Nut-Cracking Skills (Part II) created more effective relationships within the team and cross-functionally. Those relationships proved to be the key to successfully implementing change, and improving overall performance.

In my experience, technical organizations often don't do enough to cultivate or foster interpersonal communication skills. Teams that are competent in planning, building, and running systems and networks place high value on "hard" technical skills. Interpersonal communication, regarded as a "soft" skill, is not as highly valued and is often missing. Unfortunately, without this skill, effective relationships do not exist. Individual and team potential is hindered, and optimal performance of the overall organization is never realized. Imagine what would happen if that changed? What might happen if everyone intentionally acted to connect in a meaningful way with their colleagues? How much more efficient, productive, and successful could an organization become if each person forged effective relationships?

It's a challenge to establish meaningful connections in our nutty world. We have increasing demands and commitments for work, family, faith community, philanthropy, etc. Furthermore, there are other phenomena in our modern day significantly impacting interpersonal communication, our ability to adapt to one another, and the effectiveness of personal and professional relationships. These include: 1) communication technology; internet, email, cell phones, social networking (discussed next), and 2) generational differences (discussed later in this chapter). However, forging meaningful connections and effective relationships with our fellow nuts is simple once you understand and adapt to these phenomena, and begin applying the Nut-Cracking Skills.

The Quick Hits

John's innocent habit of keeping the Caps Lock key on demonstrates how technology has changed the communication landscape, substituting electronic methods for communicating in person or over the phone. Have you ever seen ten-plus emails with the same subject line flying around with ten-plus recipients responding, causing mass confusion and mass frustration? Have you ever had a fight via text? There may not be visible bruises, but words can pack a punch! Or how about being the subject of a conversation, in which you're not included, on social media? Here's a good one from my personal archives:

One night, while sitting on my sofa surfing the Net, I received a flurry of emails from friends and family asking whether my boyfriend (now husband) and I eloped. Even my dear parents, feeling left out of such a momentous life decision, questioned me. This all started because of a picture posted to my sister's Facebook page. Someone tagged me in it using my boyfriend's last name. I'm not even on Facebook! I was initially very surprised by how quickly the false story developed and spread, and then upset by the chaos and emotional impact created from a seemingly innocent picture and comment on a social media platform which I didn't even use. It was absolutely nuts!

The rapid advancement in technology, plus rise and adoption of social media have influenced the way we connect and communicate with each other. First, there is (what I think of as) naked communication, or simply sending a message devoid of verbal and non-verbal clues, which may or may not receive a response or be correctly understood (e.g. text, email, instant message). These can certainly be effective if used as intended—for a quick hit; to ask a quick question, provide a quick answer, or quickly share information. However, they are too frequently overused as a replacement for a meeting or discussion, which is dangerous because the idea, intent, or emotion can be mistakenly sent, miscommunicated by the sender, or misunderstood by the recipient (like the emails from John SHOUTING at people), all causing a communication breakdown.

The other Quick Hit is social networking: posting messages (photos, video, text, etc.) to a group in a virtual-media environment currently popular, like Facebook, Twitter, LinkedIn, Instagram, Snapchat, etc. These communication platforms present info to multiple recipients, and may or may not elicit a response. Although I consider myself more of an anti-social networker by choice (I'm still one of the few people I know who doesn't Tweet or share Snap stories), I do recognize benefits and importance for others to more quickly connect and widely share information.

A study released in September, 2017, found that, globally, about thirty percent of the time we collectively spend online is with social media.[1] These platforms bridge distances between family and friends, enable businesses to more fully interact with customers, and broadcasters to share information with the public during an emergency, etc. The ease and convenience of these platforms makes them very useful and attractive.

However, they can also become addictive and quickly replace face-to-face or voice-to-voice communication. And because they do not provide the sender and receiver(s) simultaneous benefits of verbal and non-verbal data points, they can trigger confusion—like a Facebook page stirring up chatter that I had eloped! Or much worse, they can become a door for someone to hide behind to inflict harm. Have you, your family, or friends been victims of phishing schemes, cyber-bullying, or online predatory behavior? If not, no doubt you've heard about it.

The number of Twitter Followers, Facebook Friends, LinkedIn Connections, etc. are simply activity badges. These interactions don't provide the benefits of interpersonal communication and do not equate to real, effective relationships. We need to constantly be mindful of how we and others use rapidly evolving technology as methods of communication and the effect it has on our relationships.

The Age Game

A young law school graduate attended his first corporate closed-door meeting with several seasoned leaders. Something shocking happened. The young attorney's phone rang in the meeting … and he answered it! The reaction from the other participants in the meeting was total disbelief. First, everyone knows to put a cell phone on silent during a meeting; and second, if you must answer it, step out of the meeting. Well, evidently everyone knew this except the young lawyer. He was swiftly signaled to step out of the meeting and was later questioned, "What were you doing? What was so important that you disrupted the meeting to answer your phone?" The young man was extremely embarrassed. He was completely unaware of the cell phone norms in the company. In his experience, it was normal and perfectly acceptable to answer your phone regardless of the environment, because people are expected to be constantly connected!

This might be shocking, it might sound nutty, but it's a true story. Now you may be shaking your head, thinking, "Come on, there is no excuse for that nut to not know better." Given many years of corporate experience, that was my initial reaction too. But why would we assume he should know this? Norms develop with environmental influencers and experience, so perhaps he hadn't yet been exposed to a situation where his norm of constant connection was not acceptable. This anecdote illustrates the impact generational differences carry, and the importance of awareness and adaptation to them—for both employees and employers. Emerging generations grow up in new, ever-changing environments compared to previous generations. They more freely and easily embrace the attributes of their existing environment: music, fashion, television, technology, ideas, and attitudes of pop culture, forming a unique set of norms and values.

As we work to understand each other, or Know the Nut, it is important to maintain an awareness of differences and think about how we can better adapt to one another. A new employee, like the attorney, certainly has a responsibility to learn the corporate culture norms within his environment. However, companies also have responsibility to introduce, or on-board, employees into their environment. Awareness of, and actively addressing norms that may not align, fosters a more positive work atmosphere. In this case, a simple "No Cell Phones" sign outside of the meeting room would have introduced this norm to the attorney, which could have prevented the distraction of the phone call and likely negative judgements from his colleagues.

Norms and Values

The following table lists the most prevalent generations right now and some examples of their associated norms and values.[2,3] Date ranges are generalized and vary by report, and there are always exceptions. For those born on the cusp, it's a crapshoot; they may identify with both, parts of each, or one of them more than the other. These are not hard-and-fast rules, just guidance we can use for context. The important takeaway is to recognize that there are significant generational differences, which are influenced by our ever-changing, ever-evolving environment. Understanding and adapting to these differences helps us connect with one another:

Generation	Norms and Values
Baby Boomers 1946 - Mid 1960s	Abundance, Hardwork, Teamwork, Nuclear Family
Gen X mid-1960s - late 1970s/ Early 1980s	Latchkey Kids, Blended Families, Adaptability, Independence, Technology (PCs, cell phones, internet)
Gen Y, Millennials, "Echo Boomers," E-Generation late 1970s/early 1980s up to 2000	Everybody Wins, Social Responsibility, Teamwork, Tech Savvy, Constant Connection (high speed internet, smart devices, social media)
Gen Z, iGeneration, Gen Tech, Gen Wii, Net Gen, Gen Next, Post Gen Late 1990s onward	(Obviously still evolving at this time) Sense of Self, Optimism, Constant Connection, Tech Experts, Global, Virtualization

I'm a Gen X'er. The stories shared below shed some light on growing up in that generation. My experiences are vastly different from my parents (Baby Boomers) and my kids (Gen Z, like the attorney). I invite you to think about your environment growing up. How might your experiences differ from those of your family, friends, or colleagues?

Latchkey Kid

My parents both worked, so I cared for my little sister, Kelly, after school. I admired both of my parents for being hardworking and successful in their careers. They modeled how I wanted to be, and influenced me in the values of hard work and achievement. I didn't mind being a "latchkey" kid, except when I forgot my house key and had to break in through the kitchen window, which happened more times than I'd like to admit! The screen frame eventually developed a convenient bend, making access much easier.

I learned how to be responsible for others, entrusted with the care of my kid sister for a couple hours each day. Not to say that I was awesome in this role; I was bossy and probably not as attentive as I should have been. I was a teenager after all, with competing demands of party line, MTV, and boys, of course. But the independence, responsibility, and sense of purpose I developed caring for Kelly ultimately became part of my inner nut.

Technology!

I also grew up with rotary, pulse-dial telephones. For the benefit of later generations that haven't seen the many makes and models, ours was connected to the wall and included a large handset attached to a base with an excessively long cord (prone to knots and tangles) to allow several feet of mobility. I witnessed the technological advancement to corded touch tone, and then cordless phones (we could talk and walk around the house, or even outside)! Those who have experienced only later technology (mobile phones and smart devices) are filled with wonder at these early telecommunications devices.

Life was a mix of anticipation and anxiety. We didn't know what was going on unless we were near a phone, radio, or TV. There was no live streaming on a mobile device for Michael Jackson's epic "Thriller" video, but I remember exactly where I was, and the floor console TV I was watching when it debuted on MTV in 1983!

I didn't know who might have called until I got home or checked in from a friend's house (I hoped that my dad didn't answer the phone when the cute boy from the pool finally called me!). And, we had to take turns using the telephone. I remember pacing outside of my parent's bedroom waiting to hear one of them hang up the phone so I could finally call my BFF about… well, I'm not really sure, but it was something that occupied us for hours. Luckily, all of those issues were resolved with the invention of the smartphone!

The Computer

I remember when I was first introduced to computers in elementary school. They were giant machines: TV meets typewriter. My earliest memory was navigating the "Oregon Trail," a horrible, terrible game (because I could never win). If you ever finished the game—evading death from snakebites, drowning, typhoid fever, or a number of other maladies—you could change the program to something fun. I watched other kids who successfully completed the trail of torture, and were given permission to swap over to some other floppy-disk games (the first disks really were floppy).

Once my parents secured a home computer, an early generation IBM PC (thanks to my aunt who worked for Big Blue), I could finally experience something other than the Oregon Trail (of Torture). It had a small green screen; no icons, apps, or cool graphics. It was mostly a word processor, but we had a couple games on disks, like "Wheel of Fortune," showcasing Vanna White robotically marching across the bottom of the screen to a tinny, mechanical rendition of the game-show jingle.

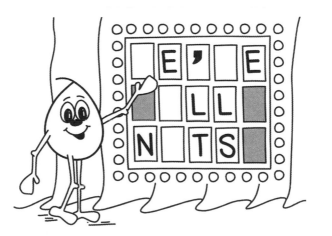

Several years later, when the Internet emerged to mainstream America, we got a new high-tech computer with a modem that "dialed up" over the telephone line and produced a static, multi-tone ear-scratching sound to reach the World Wide Web! Like any new whiz-bang invention, everyone had to pay—a lot—to use it. Internet service provider America Online (AOL) got us hooked by sending a CD with free minutes, after which we could continue surfing if we bought more minutes (which now sounds nuts)! When new and improved methods of connecting emerged, no longer limiting our minutes, many people repurposed these CDs as coffee table coasters. Gosh, suddenly I feel ancient.

The Gift of Technology and Generations

What better time to observe these modern-day challenges of technology and generational differences than during holidays and other special occasions (e.g. birthdays, baby and bridal showers, graduation and retirement parties)?

Family, friends, and colleagues of all ages gather to engage in celebration and merriment! Or maybe this is the more accurate reality: The younger kid factions are on their smartphones playing games, texting friends, watching YouTube videos, taking selfies, tracking and updating Instagram and Snap stories, while the older adult factions are totally stressed out with too many commitments, responding to work issues, and sharing chunks of precious time with some people they'd rather avoid. At the same time, the adults are telling the kids to "Get off that phone and act like you're having fun here or I'll take it away!"

As a kid, I didn't have the cool technology with which to escape my stressed-out parents or the overall nuttiness (and often sheer boredom) of these celebrations. Looking back, I realize that having a smartphone would have been awesome. Now that I belong to the adult faction, I try to be more understanding!

To set the stage for effective relationship building, be aware of the Quick Hits—when and how to use them, and the Age Game—recognizing and adapting to differing norms and values. The following Nut-Cracking Skills will further help you make connections and forge the relationships that will enhance your personal and professional success. Let's get cracking!

Part II

Nut Cracking Skills

Chapter Three

Skill 1: Know Your Nut

I was meeting with a union leader who had some issues with a team I recently acquired. I let him know my goal was to work through the issues and establish a solid partnership. As we discussed our respective approaches to the people challenges, I offered the metaphor, people are nuts, and how cracking the nut is the first step in building an effective relationship. He thought for a moment, smiled, then declared, "I'm a coconut; tough and hard to crack!" We both laughed. It was a perfect ice breaker, softening his mood and "cracking" his tough demeanor.

Serious topics, like relationships, are more approachable when examined in a not-so-serious way. That's why using nuts—often associated with fun and positive things, unless you're allergic—as a metaphor works so well. In order to crack an actual nut, you have to know the nut. Since nuts are all different and unique, proper cracking may require certain tools and techniques to get to the kernel, or the inner nut, without making a major mess.

The shell might be fiercely protective, like that of a coconut or macadamia (both require a special technique and tool). Or it may be less protective, like a peanut shell (all you need are fingers). People, like nuts, are all different and unique; to build effective relationships, we first need to "crack the nut." Our persona is the protective outer shell, which encases our inner self: our inner nut. Protection of our inner nut is often situational, depending on how open we are or want to be, or how easily we trust others.

Human Nut Types

If we think about the people we encounter, we can establish classifications, or Human Nut Types. The intent is not to stereotype, which presents (unfounded) assumptions, inhibits our curiosity, and prevents further discovery. Rather, the intent is to have a heightened awareness of how people are, drawing on previous experiences with similar nut types, to identify attributes and quickly adapt our style (select the nut-cracking tool) and make a connection (crack the nut). To truly Know the Nut, we need to use interpersonal communication skills, and active listening. Active listening, which we'll explore in Chapter Five: Give the Present of Presence, is simply tuning into and interpreting verbal and non-verbal messages to get to know our audience.

In this section, I will introduce five nut types as examples: Narcissist, Enthusiastic Extrovert, Quiet Introvert, Ambivert, Suspicious/Paranoid, and Disengaged. I've described how I see these human nuts; you may have a different perspective, and that's okay. The point is to consciously notice how people are—which can change—so that we can attempt to adapt to them, complement (or harmonize with) their style, and make a connection.

Narcissist

"Narcissists don't really want friends, because that requires work. What they really want are fans, followers, and worshippers."

-Anonymous

Narcissist Nate

Colleagues Sandy and Jane attended a seminar with dozens of other professionals from around the country. Although the attendees all shared in a similar profession, most were not acquainted. During the seminar, attendees were assigned breakout groups, and the two women were grouped with Nate. Nate was fit, a sharp dresser, and a real talker; he immediately took charge, monopolizing the discussion with his ideas. It was clear he thought they should just listen to him since he had such an amazing career, glowing reputation, and innumerable successes. When someone did manage to get a word or two in, he'd interrupt and one-up with an astounding achievement to showcase his brilliance. When the break-out activity was over, Jane whispered to Sandy as they walked away, "Wow, that guy was a complete jerk!"

A true narcissist is self-absorbed, self-involved, center-focused, defensive, or angered by critique, and views himself as a victim when things don't go his way. This nut lacks emotional intelligence and isn't concerned with investing time to build effective relationships. Why would he need you, since everybody needs him? He might truly believe he's a genius and will tell you why all day long, or preferably have you to tell him why. If he trusts that you know how great and important he is, and that you won't cross him, he'll let you into his world. But, expect to get the short end of the stick with this human nut. A relationship with a true narcissist is not reciprocal, fulfilling, or mutually beneficial. In fact, it's an ineffective relationship. If we think otherwise, we'll soon realize we were nuts!

I believe I have known a couple of true narcissists. But I also believe there aren't a lot of them. We may be quick to arrive at that judgement because of their appearance and associated stereotypes: extremely fit and attractive, dressed in expensive clothes and jewelry, and talks incessantly about themselves. However, over time we might find our initial impression was totally wrong. The story of Nate hasn't ended yet. Below, Sandy sees Nate in a whole new way.

Nate – Not actually a Narcissist

A few months after the seminar, Sandy attended another, much smaller event. She saw Nate, and as her luck would have it, she was seated at his table. This time, he had a friend with him and introduced the two. Over the next hour, the previously-pegged "complete jerk" was jovial, funny, and conversed openly without monopolizing or one-upping, and Nate and Sandy both shared some very personal experiences. Sandy found she not only liked him but actually admired him. They ended up building a friendship and an effective relationship over time. Nate became a great supporter and professional mentor to Sandy.

In these stories, Nate's behavior was different between events; what was the difference? Maybe he was more comfortable in the smaller venue. Maybe he didn't feel pressure to prove himself because he was with a friend. Only Nate truly knows. But since Sandy was willing to interact with him again, she got to know a very different person from her initial impression and built an effective relationship.

Enthusiastic Extrovert

"I desperately need people. I recharge by sitting near those I love, laughing at their antics, and sharing stories. Being by myself is exhausting."

-Unknown Extrovert

> ### *Extroverted Erin*
>
> *Erin is one of the busiest women on the planet. She is a wife, a mom, and a wildly successful career woman. Erin is heavily involved with the local community, participates on boards, and is an active philanthropist. She is a foodie who loves to cook and enjoys throwing parties for any occasion. On a rare night without plans, she will spontaneously invite friends over to reconnect and enjoy a delicious meal she created. Erin truly finds new energy, contentment, and happiness in spending as much time as possible with others.*

Comfortable to be just about anywhere with anyone, this nut never has a shortage of plans. She knows everyone and is easy to engage in conversation. If you are not this human nut type, then I'd suggest seeking them out at seminars, networking events, or large social venues where you'd rather not be; you'll immediately feel less isolated. Some may initially question this nut's sincerity. However, trust is very important to her. It is an essential component to building an effective relationship with this nut because of everyone in her life. She appreciates authentic connections and knows she can rely on those she trusts when something really matters. If you're not an extrovert, serious effort is required to keep up with this nut since non-extroverts don't naturally match her energy level!

Quiet Introvert

"Solitude matters, and for some people, it's the air they breathe."

-Susan Cain

Ian the Introvert

Ian is a graphic designer. He loves his job and works late into the night improving his skills and learning how to do more cool stuff. He's a thinker—a very deep, sometimes over-thinker—of things. Ian has many acquaintances, but he only considers a few select people very good, trusted friends. He will sometimes go out, but he doesn't enjoy new people very much (they are mostly annoying). When he's out he is consumed by thoughts: Who are these people? Where did they come from? Why are they here? What are they thinking? It's very exhausting for him. He needs time away from the pressure of the immediate moment; away from the chatter, the noise, and the annoying people. Ian prefers to be alone to consider possibilities and make sense of the vast world around him.

This private nut doesn't freely share, but rather observes. He prefers to skip the small talk, but appreciates true, authentic connections. He's a deep thinker, a philosopher who enjoys deep, meaningful conversations. Introverts seek solitude and prefer written communication (email, traditional letters, or texting) over a phone call. Connecting in person is most effective one-on-one, or in very a small group. To successfully build an effective relationship with this nut, respect his space and establish trust.

Ambivert

"Life is a struggle of constantly wanting to go out and have fun with people and also simultaneously trying to avoid all human contact."

-Anonymous Ambivert

Ambivert Amy

People are drawn to Amy. She is kind, fun, reliable, and always willing to help someone in need. She has a loving family, an expansive network of great friends, and is a "go-to" person at work, never turning down a request. She prizes her family, friends, and colleagues, however at times Amy feels lost and disconnected from herself. She has many important ideas for innovation and invention that she is tugged to pursue as part of her purpose and unique identity. Her life is a delicate balance of being and doing with others versus being and doing alone.

These nuts are chameleons. They excel at changing their persona to "play the part" and are adept at adapting to their environment. For example, an ambivert might be mistaken for an extrovert initially; like at a dinner party with close friends, leader of a team or organization, or captain of a fundraiser. They are genuinely outgoing and gregarious at times; however, they also require solitude to refuel and feel balanced. They might seem flaky (not committing to an invitation, or falling through on a commitment) due to their ongoing conflict to socialize, or to be alone. But don't stop inviting them! Although they may waffle, an invite is a compliment and they are deeply appreciative of the thought. Getting to know this nut requires keen observation, respecting their space and need for flexibility, and ongoing positive rapport to keep them interested. Building an effective relationship requires trust.

Suspicious / Paranoid

"Stay paranoid and trust no one."

-Unknown

Suspicious Sam

"I'm here to help you and the team" Sam's new boss said with an all-too-easy smile. Sam's company was in the midst of a merger and his team had been reorganized, resulting in a new boss and who-knows-what else. He'd been in this situation many times before. As he sat in his boss's office, arms crossed and expressionless, all Sam could do was play out what was about to happen next. His boss said his goal was to learn everything about the new team so that he could "help out," but Sam was certain his new boss's true motive was to gather enough intelligence needed to send everyone packing. Layoffs were coming.

This nut is running low on trust. He often shows up during times of change. He has formed a strong outer shell to protect his inner nut, and must feel trust and confidence in another before he'll share much about himself. There is a "probation" period with him; he needs evidence that you are trustworthy. Expect that it will take extra time and effort to crack this nut; however, it is achievable! Provide opportunities for regular interaction, like getting together one-on-one. Be open and share your own relevant stories and experiences. Show that you trust and value him by seeking his thoughts and input for important decisions. Eventually, he will have the evidence he needs and his protective shell will crack!

Disengaged

"Please cancel my subscription to your issues."

-*Anonymous*

> ### *Disengaged Daisy*
>
> *It has been seven years. Some say it's the seven-year itch, but Daisy realizes they just aren't meant to be together. Actually, they couldn't be more different. She is a Virgo, he is Gemini; incompatible signs, so there you go. In the beginning, right out of college, things were fun; they went out, saw friends, were just starting their careers—life was exciting! But now he is always working; late hours at the office, business trips, and constantly on-call. In his spare time, he and his buddies tinker with cars. He doesn't want to go anywhere with her. Daisy is bored and feels unimportant. She wants adventure, excitement, and fun. The attraction is gone and precious time is wasting away in this relationship. Getting out now would be good for both of them.*

Trust is gone: trust that she'll have fun with her spouse again, trust that a friend has her back, trust that a leader will make the right decisions, and so on. This nut is just "over it"—disconnected, checked out—and may also be a Negative Nellie with a penchant for bringing others down. Trust that was once there but degraded, or gone completely, will take tremendous effort and desire to rebuild, if it's even possible. There's history, probably unpleasant, that this human nut needs to accept and overcome in order to establish or reestablish meaningful connections. This nut will often avoid or terminate parts or all of the offending relationship, although coaching or counseling may help to salvage it. For example, coaching a disengaged employee may uncover an opportunity for him to reengage and be successful in the company. Or a couple may seek counseling to work through an issue threatening a break-up. However, these interventions won't always work, and the nuts might need to just move on.

🌰🌰🌰

These profiles are not an authoritative declaration of fact. They are human nut type examples from my own experiences. Maybe you'd change the descriptions I used, and maybe you'd add others. That's totally okay. The point is to be aware of the type of nut you're talking to so that you know how to crack it.

Through interpersonal communication and active listening, you'll have a quick sense, whether it's a first encounter or someone you've known for a long time, of the nut type with whom you're interacting. Be mindful of those non-verbal cues; they are clues that expedite the analysis:

❖ *Is she sitting tall and "open" or crouched and "closed"? More likely extrovert or introvert, respectively.*

❖ *Is she scowling or frowning? She may be suspicious / paranoid.*

❖ *Is she rolling her eyes, smirking, looking down? She may be disengaged.*

Use EQ to process the data points you pick up, then refer to previous experiences with similar nuts to more quickly and easily connect with this one: What type of nut is he? How does he communicate? What matters to him? How can I adapt my style to complement his?

Nut-cracking also requires trust. Each human nut type I've described, even the narcissist, requires trust to connect. Openness and authenticity builds trust. Trust encourages mutual sharing, enabling connection points from which an effective relationship can be built.

Chapter Four

Skill 2:
Give the Present of Presence

A friendly lady, enjoying a cup of tea on a beautiful summer afternoon, watched from a curbside bistro table as a mom and her four-year old daughter walked around town. Mom was a seasoned multitasker, running her errands while "working" furiously on her smartphone with daughter in tow. The little girl chatted to herself as she followed Mom to the library, resigned to the fact that her mom's undivided attention was given to the "crack-phone" in her hands (neither of which was available for her daughter to hold).

The little girl noticed the stranger at the table, smiled and waved, prompting a reciprocal response from the friendly lady. When they emerged from the library, Mom was still consumed with something fascinating on her phone, head down, relying on anything but her eyes to navigate the road and sidewalk— it's questionable if she even knew whether her daughter was still behind her. They made a second stop at the Post Office, and then headed to their car. Mom was laughing out loud at something hilarious shared by whoever was on the other end of the phone. The little girl again spotted the lady at the table, gave another smile, and waved goodbye. Her mom never noticed (or at least acknowledged) the lady, or the exchanges with her daughter.

There are many forces competing for our time and attention. We live in an environment inundated by technology. Our devices, smartphones, smart TVs, tablets and Apple watches enable constant "connection" to virtually anyone or anything, anytime. To build effective relationships, we need to show others that we value and care about them. Showing that we care requires us to be fully present in our interactions. How much time do you and people you know spend on social media? How disciplined are you in removing distractions when you're interacting with your kids, spouse, colleagues, friends? It's easy to criticize the mom in this story for being self-absorbed and inattentive to her daughter. However, when we consider the environment we live in and honestly think about our own habits (influenced by increased expectations about constant electronic connection), we might be surprised to realize we exhibit similar behavior.

Have you ever been out with friends and noticed, after looking up, that everyone is staring into their phones?

Have you gone through a checkout lane and ignored the cashier because you were talking to someone on the phone?

Have you been in a meeting where everyone has their phones and laptops for a "working session," but you're secretly conducting unrelated business: paying a bill, managing your email, or checking the score of a game?

In any of these examples, we're quick to decide a person is rude, self-absorbed, inattentive, or a bad mom (we hope that's not really the case). The fact is we have a rapidly increasing affinity for the technology that serves our social media addiction, brought on by an unquenchable thirst to know what is happening around us at all times, compounded by expectations that we are always available and 'in-the-know'. The addiction, thirst, and expectations hi-jack time and attention for interpersonal communication.

Social Media

An eye-opening study that was released in January, 2017, by SocialMediaToday.com,[1] aimed at marketing education, used average-time-spent-per-day on some of the most popular platforms (YouTube, Facebook, Snapchat, Instagram, Twitter) to project the amount of time an average person will spend on social media over their lifetime:

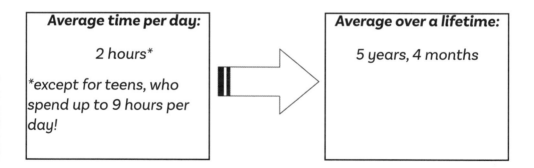

The research built on this by comparing the time spent on social media to that of typical daily activities (based on current data), over a lifetime:

Watching TV:	7 years, 8 months
Social Media:	5 years, 4 months
Eating and Drinking:	3 years, 5 months
Grooming:	1 year, 10 months
Socializing:	1 year, 3 months
Doing Laundry:	6 months

The study then took it one step further, identifying outstanding feats a person could accomplish with the same amount of time spent on social media in a lifetime (5 years and 4 months). Here are my favorites:

*Fly to the moon and back **32 times***

*Walk the Great Wall of China **3.5 times***

*Climb Mt. Everest **32 times***

As the research points out, people spend a whole lot of time on social media—and it's growing. So, what's the solution? If our goal is to build deeper, more effective relationships, then we need to seize opportunities to dedicate ourselves to this pursuit. This requires awareness of how we're currently spending our time—perhaps setting boundaries on our use of social media to interact—and intentionally using interpersonal, face-to-face communication whenever possible.

Time

Time is precious; everyone knows it and feels it. We have many demands on our time: meetings, boss(es), colleagues, adminis-trivia, family, friends, school, sports, faith activities, volunteer ac-tivities, and on and on. When those 7 a.m. or 5 p.m. meetings pop into the calendar do you think, as I do: Are you kidding me? You were hoping to get an early workout in, or finally get to that hair appointment you've had to reschedule for the last two months. Perhaps you're just getting ready to leave work but need to finish a last, hard-thought email response, or complete the flashy touches on a presentation for tomorrow, or rush out the door to make the parent-teacher conference. Right at that very moment your boss "pops" you on IM with twenty questions about your project, or an upset employee walks into your office to lodge a complaint, or your phone rings and it's the customer you've been trying to reach all day. Feelings of great annoyance emerge. We could ig-nore the interruption, or go nuts and lash out over it. Although

these are among our options (which I might have selected once
or twice), either route will more likely create problems for us; irri-
tate the boss, further upset the employee, or anger the customer.
On the other hand, reframing the interruption as an opportunity
and choosing to give our time to the person seeking us out, shows
him that he is valued and important. It's okay to say "Give me a few
minutes to finish up here and I'll call you back shortly." Bolstering
feelings of value and importance fosters trust, promoting a deeper,
more effective relationship.

Attention

Paula, a psychiatric nurse, sat across from her patient conducting an assessment in a small room with the lulling buzz of a fluorescent light fixture overhead. Paula was extremely tired from working long hours on an erratic schedule. She propped up her head on her fist, supported by her elbow, struggling to stay awake. She made a periodic note for the record while listening to the woman in front of her. Paula's patient was an obese, older woman who spoke in a soft, breathy style, pausing frequently as she incoherently droned on and on. The rambling story came to an abrupt stop and the nurse suddenly jolted, realizing she'd drifted off to a lovely dream state for a few seconds. Momentarily lost and disorientated, Paula asked her patient the first question that popped into her head, "When did you have the gastric bypass?" The patient never had a gastric bypass. Luckily for the nurse, who was immediately mortified by her question, the patient was a certifiable crazy nut who also wasn't paying any attention!

Have you ever tuned out during a meeting or conversation, feeling completely lost, and maybe a little embarrassed? All people—sane, insane, or somewhere in between—are social creatures with an innate need to communicate and connect with others. Interpersonal communication enables us to forge effective relationships, and listening is an integral part of this process. People want to talk and will share about themselves if they know you are listening (and some even if you aren't, like the nutty patient). However, to be truly effective, we can't just passively listen but rather actively listen.

Which feels better? Talking to someone who:

(1) is staring at their phone or computer, responding to texts, Instant Messenger (IM) and emails, and occasionally looks up to ask you to, "say that again"?

OR

(2) is looking at you, turned away from distractions of IM and email. Their phone is silenced and put away, and they show genuine interest in what you're saying by participating in the conversation?

Active Listening

Active listening is not multi-tasking, looking at a computer screen, staring off into space, or struggling to stay awake (like the psychiatric nurse). Active listening is noticing eye contact (or lack of), facial expressions, body position and movement, and voice inflection. It is interpreting what you notice:

❖ *Is she looking at you with keen focus or distractedly looking away?*

❖ *Is her body position open and trusting, or closed and untrusting?*

❖ *Does her expression convey approval or disapproval?*

❖ *Does her voice carry confidence or uncertainty?*

❖ *Is she comfortably still, or nervously fidgeting?*

While doing all of this, we also remember what is actually said. We take sincere interest in the person, are curious to understand what they say and how they say it. Our interest is piqued by key words, and we may even commit to memory a nugget of trivia shared by the other nut; perhaps an interest, hobby, kids, etc., to recall and weave into future conversations as a reconnection point!

Chapter Five

Skill 3:
Possess Greater Power in Person

Julie was twenty-two years young, hired for her first big job. She was a new manager reporting to the Financial Controller of a large, global company. She had no previous finance experience, and had no idea what a Controller actually did. Julie felt like a clueless nut. Over the next few weeks, however, she noticed her boss was always in the office before she arrived (which was early because she wanted to impress) and after she left (late because, again, she wanted to impress). She soon realized her boss had a very important job; he was responsible for the productivity and profitability of the entire operation.

Despite his enormous responsibility, Julie quickly saw how much he valued his employees; he always made time for them. In addition to regular staff meetings, he scheduled recurring one-on-one sessions. Every meeting was in person, never over the phone. For meetings with the larger team, he brought everyone together in a conference room—often with snacks and coffee (later Julie learned, as a leader herself, that food helped boost meeting attendance). Smaller meetings were held in his office, but he cleared away all that he was working on to give one-hundred percent of his focus to his audience. His efforts and dedication to interact in person made Julie and her colleagues feel important and valued.

Face It

We are so consumed with full schedules and being tied to our smart devices, that interpersonal communication is needed now more than ever. Face-to-face communication has become a "Superpower" for connecting with others.

> **In person interaction is important personally and professionally for two key reasons:**
>
> 1. You will probably save time with direct, face-to-face communication because it's very hard to ignore someone standing right in front of you!
>
> 2. People get to know each other and build trust much faster.

Face-to-face communication provides the benefit of non-verbal clues: eye contact, facial expressions, body posture and position (leaning forward/backward, open vs. closed), and movement (rocking, tapping, fidgeting, nodding, shifting, etc.). Additionally, the trust factor is stronger when people can actually see each other. A study conducted in 2010 with two hundred undergraduate students showed that face-to-face contact fostered greater trust and cooperation than any other methods. Researcher and Professor Gregory Northcraft concluded that in person, ". . . people just have more confidence that others will do what they say they'll do."[1]

Today we live and operate in a global environment. Many of us have friends, family, work colleagues, and customers in different geographies, so showing up is not always possible. Although in many ways technology detracts from interpersonal communication, it has offered amazing new ways of connecting with our global community. Live video services, like Facetime, Skype,

Webex, GoToMeeting, and telepresence products, simulate face-to-face interaction when physical presence is not possible; that is super-cool technology. Northcraft's research also showed that video-conferencing, although trailing behind face-to-face interaction, was a more effective option in building trust and cooperation than email.

Unfortunately, it has become easy to get away from physically showing up in our immediate-gratification culture. Face-to-face interactions are replaced by texts, IM, Tweets, Snaps, etc. Maybe we have too many balls in the air and too little time. Yet there is no substitute for the efficacy of face-to-face, interpersonal communication. We have many more data points in person, taking the verbal and non-verbal cues (eye contact, expressions, inflection, posture, and movement) to "read" the other nut and ensure the messages between one another are clear. So make time to walk down the hall; meet for coffee or tea. Plan a Happy Hour to talk to your peeps in person instead of posting, texting, Snapchatting, Tweeting, IMing, emailing, etc. It will save time and build trust more quickly! And, if you're in a marathon of meetings, you could probably use the physical and mental break. In the context of relationship building, you will possess a nut-cracking Superpower when you proceed in person.

Chapter Six

Skill 4: Share Your Inner Nut

One summer morning I was at the park, heading back to my car after a jog. As I walked through an area that was usually deserted, I saw a woman with a Great Dane hanging out at a nearby table. I smiled, waved, and complimented her magnificent dog. She responded with a smile, and said, "He's very friendly," which I took as an invitation to go over and meet them.

I learned that her gentle giant was a service dog that routinely visited the elderly, but visits were mostly to men because the ladies were afraid of his size. "Speaking of size," I said, "my aunt used to have Komondors" (a large white

Hungarian breed with doggie dreadlocks). She knew exactly the breed I was talking about and enthusiastically shared how she used to "show" Kuvasz, another Hungarian breed.

We chatted about our love of dogs. She'd had several while she was growing up. I shared that I never had a dog as a child, despite incessantly begging and pestering my parents for one. My pet growing up was a hamster, but he tragically passed away from pneumonia after one short year of life. I was determined to get a dog, however, and at twenty-one I finally did and have had a four-legged Bestie ever since!

In about ten minutes we established a meaningful connection, and it felt like we were fast friends. Although I may not see my new friend or her dog again, I certainly won't ever forget them!

To Share . . .

Sharing encourages others to open up and for you both to find common ground to connect. Sharing demonstrates your trust in the other person, and in turn builds their trust in you. Since most people seek positive interactions and enjoy talking about themselves (and I don't mean in a narcissistic way!), it's easy to initiate the process. We cannot expect to have an effective relationship that is one-sided. For example, a new manager cannot expect a team to trust and follow her lead if they don't know anything about her past experience or professional values. We also cannot expect to turn a new acquaintance into a good friend without getting to know each other's interests, personal values, etc.

The pace and depth of sharing are situational and differ depending on the type of relationship being forged. Running into a stranger in a park is vastly different (in scale but not in process!) than building rapport in a business environment. To be a successful leader in a new team, for example, it's important to share about yourself to begin building trust: relevant job experiences, professional values, and communication style (e.g. detailed explanation vs. bottom-line approach). Offering a couple personal nuggets about your family or hobby interests will also help the team members identify with you beyond simply the boss.

Also, as a leader starting with a new team, it's a top priority to get to know the individual team members, each nut. As we saw with Julie and her boss in Chapter Six, employees feel important and valued when they have opportunities to connect, especially in person. Over time, sharing more information about yourself and personal values (family, interests, world views, etc.) happens naturally as mutual trust grows, and will strengthen the relationship.

It's remarkable how quickly people, even complete strangers, will share their inner nut, given the right setting. When I was younger, I was quite shy and reserved. I was afraid of saying the wrong thing and not being accepted. Throughout my life and career I have all but lost that fear and become very open and willing to share my inner nut. The shift came when I realized that other people have the same fears. The more open we are, the more we share, and the more quickly we connect.

. . . Or "Nut" to Share

On the other hand, be mindful of inappropriate sharing. This can make others uncomfortable and prevent the connection, scoring zero points in effective relationship building. Here is an example:

> Georgia, a friendly souvenir store owner in a small town, struck up a conversation with a father and daughter who stopped in to her shop. She proceeded to share a story about her son who found, ". . . a creepy crawler [tick] under that flap of skin, you know, that hangs from your butt over your leg." After enduring several very uncomfortable minutes politely listening to Georgia (her son was found to be in good health despite the tick incident), the visitors quickly found the nearest door to exit (without a purchase).

Oversharing or consistently redirecting the conversation to one-self will also score zero points:

> *While attending a networking event, Tom noticed a gentle-man who appeared nervous and shy. He walked up to the man, introduced himself and asked about his background. Tom immediately became mercilessly locked into a fif-teen-minute summation of the guy's current unemployment situation, his complete work history, and his career goals. Tom never said a word and was saved by an announcement for attendees to take their seats. He went to the opposite end of the room and kept a wary eye out to avoid the "shy" man for the rest of the event.*

Maybe a person is nervous, simply talking to fill awkward space. Maybe they are very eager and can't contain their excitement. Maybe they don't have a conversation filter. Whatever the case, lack of situational awareness can lead to inappropriate sharing or oversharing, and prevent the communication "dance," as described by L. Edna Rogers: ". . . how we move in relation to one another via our communication behavior [that] forms the patterns that underlie and identify our interpersonal relationships."[1] Always be mindful of when to share, and when "nut" to share!

Let's dance! In the next chapter, Engage the Nut, we'll explore how to invite your partner to the communication dance.

Chapter Seven

Skill 5: Engage the Nut

A leader was struggling to build relationships at work. He said that people didn't approach him outside of meetings, and he never engaged in conversations unrelated to the programs and initiatives he owned. He felt like people viewed him as arrogant, but in fact he was just very shy. What could he do to change how people perceived and responded to him?

The last skill—and arguably the most critical to cracking and dancing with more nuts—is engagement. This competency is especially important for the non-extrovert nut types who may struggle making connections but sincerely desire to build more relationships. In this chapter we will explore how to invite other nuts to the communication dance, enabling more connections and relationship-building through the power of smiling, recognizing and respecting differences, paying compliments, and embracing criticism!

Smile

In Chapter Seven, when the woman at the park smiled back at me, I was immediately disarmed and eager to meet her and her giant dog. The smile signaled an invitation to connect, and quickly resulted in us both sharing some of our inner nut! What makes smiling so powerful?

Smiling Makes You Appear More Approachable

What do you think about someone who smiles at you? A few things that come to mind about this person are: nice, happy, and friendly. That's a nut I'd like to know! On the other hand, how about someone who doesn't smile? I think: negative, crabby, and they have issues! I hesitate to interact with them, wondering "What's their problem?" "Will they be mean to me?" I'll probably pass on cracking that nut. Simply being aware of this might flip that frown upside down. In "The Hidden Power of Smiling" TED Talk, Ron Gutman shares several studies on the effects of smiling, including one conducted by Penn State University that found smiling makes people appear more likeable, courteous, and competent.[1] People who smile are also perceived as more attractive, reliable, relaxed, and sincere.[2] All good qualities to have for building effective relationships!

Smiling Makes You Feel Better

Do you ever find yourself clenching your teeth when you're really stressed about something? When you become aware of it, force a smile. It's a bit mystical, but try it to calm down, relax, and feel better. It works. It's scientifically proven, too. Studies show that smiling lowers stress, anxiety, and blood pressure, and promotes a longer life.[3]

Smiling is Contagious

When you see someone smiling directly at you, what do you do? It actually takes effort to not smile back.[4] When we get in a funk, sometimes we just want to wallow in our own negativity. But if some brave soul has the courage to smile at us, it might be just enough to inspire us to return the expression, and Voila! We feel better! We now have the power to positively impact other people. Smile, pass it on!

Respect Differences

A couple attended a dinner party where several of the guests were new acquaintances and eager to establish new relationships. The 2016 Presidential election was drawing near and it was a matter of minutes before the topic of politics surfaced (No!). As the guests settled in, it became immediately clear this was a mix of strong supporters on both sides. The wife was never one to engage in debate over politics or religion, knowing these were fiercely value-driven topics. She quietly observed and listened, figuring out the different types of nuts present. Her awareness—and respect of their differences—helped her navigate conversations toward areas of neutral ground, parenting and music, and avoid the land-mine topics. The nuts she met that night, despite their differences, established connections and ultimately became very close friends (but they still don't discuss politics).

Our norms and values are personal, influenced by our environment and experiences. Understanding and respecting another's norms and values is essential to establishing their sense of comfort and trust in us. Try on a different shell to see things through another nut's perspective! To connect, we do not need to agree; we just need to understand. Further, unless we are asked for input, listening and affirming is far more beneficial than offering an unsolicited opinion or feedback. There is even a chance to be awakened to a compelling new perspective. Asserting uninvited views over someone else's will shut down the communication dance and challenge—or even stop—progress toward building trust and an effective relationship.

The story in Chapter Three about the attorney who answered his cell phone during a meeting demonstrates how norms and values may differ greatly. To show we care about a relationship, whether it's personal or professional, it is important to be aware and respectful of unique differences.

Compliment

Several years ago, my husband shared the perfect metaphor with me for relationships: emotional bank accounts. You may have read this in works by Stephen Covey, John Gottman, or others, but that was the first time I'd heard this very simple and fitting metaphor. Positive interactions represent deposits into the account, while negative interactions are withdrawals out of the account. Most people prefer an account with a lot of moola; netting much higher deposits than withdrawals, and thus have greater financial security, comfort, and possibilities (what shall I buy?). Similarly, when deposits outweigh withdrawals in relationships, there is greater trust, emotional security, comfort, and possibility (mutual benefit). The higher the balance, the healthier the relationship!

Positive interactions, like compliments, don't work if they're insincere. To count, they must be meaningful to the receiving nut. Once we start looking, we can find things about anyone (even a narcissist, if we're willing) that hit the mark. Volunteering, making a donation, cooking a meal, stepping up to help a peer, defusing an explosive customer, completing chores, or a honey-do list without being asked—all fair game for a compliment! The guidance here is to more often find and call out positive behaviors and actions. Keep clarity and timeliness in mind, so that people know you're paying attention and sincerely care!

Embrace Criticism

Criticism has a bad rap. It can simply mean an analysis or assessment, or it can also mean disapproval. It is this second meaning that creates a negative reaction for people. However, because it can alert us to a problem perceived by another person, criticism may contain a helpful message to benefit us (if we choose to listen):

Criticism: *She gets more pointers about her golf swing than she actually swings.*

Problem: *She stinks at golf.*

Message: *Take lessons and practice.*

Criticism: *He receives an 'F' on the exam.*

Problem: *He was out late partying the night before, rather than studying.*

Message: *Study instead of partying next time.*

> **Criticism:** *She gets a ticket for driving 80 mph in a 40 mph zone.*
>
> **Problem:** *She drives too fast!*
>
> **Message:** *Slow down.*

In relationships, being receptive to criticism also helps us recognize a problem exists so we can work to resolve it:

> **Criticism:** *People outside of John's team think he is rude and grumpy.*
>
> **Problem:** *Using all caps in email causes people to think John is SHOUTING at them!*
>
> **Message:** *Stop using all caps (unless he really is shouting).*

> **Criticism:** *A fed up wife tells her husband she feels taken for granted around the house.*
>
> **Problem:** *The husband and kids haven't shown their appreciation lately.*
>
> **Message:** *Show her she is appreciated. Do something to surprise her, like cleaning the house and cooking a special meal!*

Criticism: *You don't respect my time or value me" (explicitly stated or implicitly conveyed through an employee's behavior)*

Problem: *Boss consistently multi-tasks during one-on-one meetings, responding to email, phone calls, and IMs.*

Message: *Give the present of presence! Remove distractions and give full focus to connect with employee(s).*

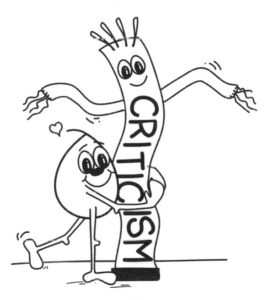

When we embrace criticism, we have an opportunity to identify actual problems and discover potential solutions, which serves us in improving our interactions and strengthening our relationships.

Chapter Eight

In a Nutshell...

The Nutty Spread

Relationships are critical to both personal and professional success. By intentionally using interpersonal communication and EQ, we interact with others in a mindful and meaningful way, enabling the meaningful connections needed to build effective relationships. Interpersonal communication has been hindered by jam-packed schedules, technology, social media, and generational gaps.

❖ *Technology enables us to be more productive and connected. The ease and convenience of these platforms makes them very useful and attractive. However, they can also become addictive and too easily replace interpersonal communication.*

❖ *Each generation grows up in new, ever-changing environments, different from their predecessors'. As a result, they form a unique set of norms and values. In order to connect with each other, we must maintain an awareness of differences and a willingness to adapt to one another.*

Become an expert nut-cracker by taking every opportunity to apply the Nut-Cracking Skills:

Skill 1: Know the Nut

Connecting, or cracking the nut, requires us to be aware of the nut type, and to adapt our communication style (select the appropriate nut-cracking tool) to complement their style. Match tone, speed of speaking, amount of sharing, movement, and expression. Always be aware of your audience, since people will change their outer shell, or persona, depending on situation, environment, and experiences.

Skill 2: Give the Present of Presence

Remove distractions and actively listen to tune into verbal and non-verbal clues. Be aware of how much time you spend on social media, where you give your attention, and how you show up (attentive/inattentive) to other nuts. Set boundaries regarding social media activity, shift your attention or make adjustments to be more attentive; it boosts presence and shows that you care and value the nuts in your life.

Skill 3: Possess Greater Power In Person

You are harder to ignore and will speed up the relationship building process with face-to-face interaction. Trust is the key ingredient to effective relationships, and is gained more quickly in person. If physical presence is not possible, consider live video technology; although it not as effective as face-to-face interaction, it provides benefits of verbal and non-verbal clues.

Skill 4: Share Your Inner Nut

Sharing encourages people to open up and find common ground to connect. The more open we are, the more we share, and the more quickly we connect—the nut is cracked. Sharing is essential to demonstrating trust for another, and in turn builds others' trust in us. Consider the type of relationship when determining the pace and depth of sharing. Be mindful of what to share and what "nut" to share!

Skill 5: Engage the Nut

Invite other nuts to the communication dance. Connect through the power of smiling, respecting differences, paying meaningful compliments, and embracing criticism to discover hidden messages.

Take the Nut-Cracking Challenge

Practicing the Nut-Cracking Skills encourages the mutual sharing and trust that build and maintain effective relationships. Think of the nut metaphor in all interactions, like a personal nut-cracking challenge with people you know: colleagues, friends, family, and people you don't know: restaurant servers, cashiers, fellow joggers or walkers at the lake. Note! This is probably a bad idea at the Target checkout on Saturday, since everyone is anxious to get through the line and idle chitchat with the cashier will drive some people nuts. Even without an intention to build a relationship, you gain skill and confidence in every connection you make, every nut you crack!

Chapter Nine

Host Your Own Nut Mixer!

Do you want to connect or reconnect with family, friends, or coworkers?

Do you want an escape from daily pressures and issues?

Do you want to inject some fun and silliness into life?

Then have a Nut Party!!

❖ *It's a zero-pressure way for people (even the kids!!) to share an experience, interact face-to-face, and get away from electronics for a few minutes, maybe more!*

❖ It's such a nutty thing to do and will provide a fun escape for everyone to simply be who they are! There are no right or wrong answers. You will gather a collection of unique, thoughtful, creative, silly, and even hilarious observations for each nut.You'll provide an experience connecting your guests, which they will share and talk about long after the party.

❖ Thinking about nuts as a metaphor for people, participants will gain insight into how to connect with others by recognizing and adapting to their unique nuttiness!

So Simple, It's Nuts!

Here's what you need:

A variety of nuts in shells

Nut-cracking implements (Note: Some nuts, like macadamias, require special tools!)

Nutty Observations worksheets (see Example in Appendix)

Clipboards and pens

Separate bowls with signage identifying the different nuts

Container for discarded shells

Optional:

> *A few tasty hors d'oeuvres, in addition to the delicious nuts for cracking and eating.*

> *Beverages to match the crowd (cocktails are great to get the creative juices flowing, but HR might frown on spirits in the workplace!).*

Instructions:

Place the bowls of different nuts (with tags to identify them) and nut-cracking tools around a large table. Equip everyone with a clipboard, pen, and Nutty Observations worksheet. Let everyone experience cracking and tasting the nuts, and observe how each nut is unique. How easy or hard it is to open? Does it taste good? Was worth it? What else comes to mind about the nut? Record thoughts.

Talk About It!

People can share their nutty responses or sit back and listen to others. Remember, zero-pressure! This is a fun and interesting exercise to imagine people with characteristics of the different nuts—nuts personified! Maybe you have artists in the room that could illustrate what the nuts might look like?

Here are some questions you can ask to keep the nutty conversations going:

What nuts were the easiest to crack? Hardest?

Did you develop a technique to crack any nuts?

What was your favorite nut? Least favorite?

What random thoughts might have popped into your head?

What surprised you?

What disappointed you?

What characteristics of the nuts are similar to people?

Do you know anyone that is like any particular nut?

What type of nut are you … today?

The Nut Party activity is surprisingly similar to how we perceive and get to know each other. Understanding and adapting to how a person is enables us to crack their shell—or persona, making a connection to their kernel—or inner self. From there, we are off to building a relationship!

Appendix

Nutty Observations!

Please describe characteristics that come to you ~ Think about look, feel, smell, sound, taste!

	Outer Shell	Kernel	Any other thoughts about this nut? For example, What would it take to crack it? When do you see this nut? How do you like this nut?
Almond			
Brazil Nut			
Cashew			
Coconut			
Hazelnut / Filbert			
Macadamia			
Peanut			

Nutty Observations!

Please describe characteristics that come to you ~ Think about look, feel, smell, sound, taste!

	Outer Shell	Kernel	Any other thoughts about this nut? For example, What would it take to crack it? When do you see this nut? How do you like this nut?
Pecan – Paper shell			
Pecan – Hard shell			
Pili Nut			
Pine Nut			
Pistachio			
Walnut			

Nuts Personified

Observations from the Original Nut Mixer

Almonds

Shell (Persona)	Kernel (Inner Self)
Looks like a gang member after a shootout; it's rough, with pockmarks and holes.	Firm, but sweet. Turns out this nut is isn't so tough or exciting under that rough exterior.
Seems opinionated and may lash out sharply with its pointy and splintery exterior.	It's not high on the awesome scale until after a good deal of preparation.
Tread carefully cracking this nut; things can get very messy, very fast. Despite its rough appearance, the shell is thinner than expected and simple to crack with the right tool and a gentle technique.	This nut is most comfortable in others' company—especially salt, cinnamon, or chocolate!

Brazil Nuts

Shell (Persona)	Kernel (Inner Self)
A uniquely odd and interesting shape, like the section of an orange. It feels rigid and unpleasant. This nut looks tough, hard, and scary. Some consider it very ugly and are turned off by its appearance.	Unexpectedly sweet and tender, and rewards those who crack it (with a big, meaty kernel). Often regarded as a jolly nut! Very few do not enjoy this nut in some way.

Cashews

Shell (Persona)	Kernel (Inner Self)
Pretty and graceful appearance, but in reality, is fiercely protective and dangerous (because the lining around the kernel contains a toxic oil!)

Most people will never have an opportunity to crack this "nut" (a good thing because it's so hostile), but will get to meet the kernel later, after all risks have been removed. | Delicate, soft, and sweet... almost too sweet (without salt)!

Pale and needs some sun. This nut is more attractive with a golden tan.

Loves a good party and is a crowd pleaser. Most people want more of this nut! |

Coconuts

Shell (Persona)	Kernel (Inner Self)
A wild one—probably stays out too late. Looks roughed-over and disorganized.	So very pleasing ... ivory and pure like snow.
Unkempt, disheveled and needs to clean up a bit; would benefit from a shower and shave.	Very light, sweet, and nourishing. This nut sweeps you away to vacationland!
Thick shell and very hard, but warm it up a little and it begs to be cracked.	

Hazelnuts / Filberts

Shell (Persona)	Kernel (Inner Self)
Showy and impressive. A snappy dresser in beautiful earth tones.	Need to get past the thick skin before getting to the actual kernel.
Compact, hard body, yet thin shell that's relatively easy to crack.	An earthy nut. Grounded and not over-the-top. Pleasantly tasty and regarded as a good nut with a soft and chewy core; this nut will stick with you.
Often mistakenly identified (as an acorn or macadamia).	

Macadamia Nuts

Shell (Persona)	Kernel (Inner Self)
Nature's malted milk ball. Smooth operator; this perfectly formed, beautiful nut has a reputation of decadence and vanity. Be advised: this is the hardest nut to crack, requiring a specific tool and technique to attain the kernel without harming it.	Very soft and sensitive inside, with a complex sweetness. This nut is substantial and gratifying. Enriched by others, macadamias are happy nuts who enjoy giving and sharing the finer things in life.

Peanuts

Shell (Persona)	Kernel (Inner Self)
Sexually charged, resembling male anatomy! Thin, easy-to-crack shell isn't too worried about protecting the kernel. Confident in self. Always unique and unpredictable in how he'll show up, or with whom, but is fun-loving and ready to party.	Unexpected . . . You think you know how it will taste, then surprise! It has a raw, green, veggie-flavor, like a snow pea. He's okay au natural but needs to work on himself before going out to live up to expectations and be more appealing to the masses. The nut loves everyone and is a common guest at many venues—bars, ballgames, circuses, parties—but not everyone loves him; some have serious allergies to this fun-loving nut.

Hard Shell Pecans

Shell (Persona)	Kernel (Inner Self)
More masculine than others. Smooth talker, but hard, guarded, and unapproachable. This nut comes across like a showboating prize fighter.	Complicated, alluring, and takes a lot of patience and prying to understand it. The kernel does not carry the type of reward you might expect from such a difficult nut. It's unique and distinct flavor does not sit well with everyone. You might not want to go there again.

Paper Shell Pecans

Shell (Persona)	Kernel (Inner Self)
Not very strong, but beautiful, attractive, and pleasing shape. This nut has a distinctive aroma (like coffee or cocoa), but a very offensive, bitter shell.	The kernel is complex and bold. A person needs to crack this nut with care and precision to get fully past the shell and coax out the kernel, which is brainy, delicate, and widely appreciated. The convictions of this nut are strong. It has integrity and is well-respected, but not always embraced (except in pecan pie).

Pili Nuts

Shell (Persona)	Kernel (Inner Self)
Long and elegant, but has a hard and stony appearance. This nut gets to the point, and cracking it takes a straightforward, direct approach ... Whack!	After this nut is cracked, you may initially be met with a harsh and off-putting cover before reaching the uncomplicated, unassuming kernel. This is a soft, tender-hearted nut, and thought of by some as a bland, oily wuss. However, it is actually a powerhouse when it comes to health and wellness.

Pine Nuts

Shell (Persona)	Kernel (Inner Self)
Dark and mysterious.

This tiny nut is deceptively difficult to crack; it is stubborn and some may give up on this small, but mighty, gem. | Very small. May seem a little bitter… maybe resentment for those who give up on cracking it. This nut knows its worth.

Once cracked it packs a punch of flavor, while maintaining a humble elegance. It is highly regarded by those who relish a challenge to get to the prize. |

Pistachios

Shell (Persona)	Kernel (Inner Self)
Very open, inviting, high energy, and exudes personality. This nut is quick to trust, showing its kernel and making it vulnerable.	Transparency reigns with this nut—you see what you get.
	The kernel is bright, colorful, happy, playful and fun.
It's extreme openness, energy and big personality can seem intimidating. Is it coming after me with its sharp open mouth? Will this nut bite me??	This is a very social nut, loves to mingle with its own kind, loves salt, and dabbles in culinary dishes. However, the pistachio can also stand solidly on its own.
Others may judge it as a real talker: Will this nut ever shut up and listen?	

Walnuts

Shell (Persona)	Kernel (Inner Self)
This nut looks formidable; big, bold, intimidating, stubborn, and strong-willed.

The walnut is wrinkly, rough and looks a little haggard—it's been through a lot and maybe fallen on some hard times.

Despite its size and appearance, this nut entices us to crack it by giving an audible preview to its kernel with a rapid shake. It is easy to crack with persistence and a little pressure. It looks much harder to crack than it really is. | The kernel is artfully built; substantial, yet soft, and is very willing to come out. Once out of its shell, it is brainy, intellectual, and has many facets.

A unique taste that is not for everyone, but is definitely nostalgic for the holidays. |

Notes

Chapter 1: The Importance of Real (Effective) Relationships

1. Fisher, B. A., & Adams, K. L. (1994). *Interpersonal Communication – Pragmatics of Human Relationships*. McGraw-Hill, Inc., p. 1

2. Salovey, P. & Mayer, J.D. (1990). *Emotional intelligence. Imagination, Cognition, and Personality*, 9(3), 185-211.

Chapter 2: Modern-Day Challenges

1. Young, K. (2017, September 11). "Social Media Captures Over 30% of Online Time." Retrieved from globalwebindex: http://blog.globalwebindex.net/chart-of-the-day/social-media-captures-30-of-online-time/

2. Alliance Staff LLC. (n.d.). "Generation Motivations." Retrieved from Alliance Staff LLC: http://www.alliancestaff.com/employers/generation-motivations/

3. WJSchroer Company. (n.d.). "Generations X,Y, Z and the Others." Retrieved from WJSchroer: http://socialmarketing.org/archives/generations-xy-z-and-the-others/

Chapter 4: Give the Present of Presence

1. Asano, E. (2017, January 4). "How Much Time Do People Spend on Social Media?" Retrieved from SocialMediaToday: https://www.socialmediatoday.com/marketing/how-much-time-do-people-spend-social media-infographic

Chapter 5: Possess Greater Nut-Cracking Power In person

1. Dennis, J. (2010, June 16). "Relying Too Much on E-Mail Bad for Business, Study Says." Retrieved from Illinois News Bureau: https://news.illinois.edu/blog/view/6367/205605

Chapter 6: Share Your Inner Nut

1. L. Edna Rogers, P. (1989). Sixteenth Annual Student Conference in Communication. (P. L. Edna Rogers, Performer) California State University, Fresno, CA, USA.

Chapter 7: Engage the Nut

1. Gutman, R. (2011, March). "The Hidden Power of Smiling." Retrieved from TED Ideas worth spreading: https://www.ted.com/talks/ron_gutman_the_hidden_power_of_smiling

2. NeuroNation. (n.d.). "Why You Need to Smile More." Retrieved from NeuroNation: https://www.neuronation.com/science/benefits-of-smiling

3. NeuroNation. (n.d.). "Why You Need to Smile More." Retrieved from NeuroNation: https://www.neuronation.com/science/benefits-of-smiling

4. Gutman, R. (2011, March). "The hidden power of smiling." Retrieved from TED Ideas worth spreading: https://www.ted.com/talks/ron_gutman_the_hidden_power_of_smiling

A few great articles on the impact of relationships, engagement, and success:

Business2Community: http://www.business2community.com/human
-resources/workplace-relationships-lifeblood-culture-engagement
-01177667#yxU2TYl2m9OCU3B7.97

Gallup: http://www.gallup.com/businessjournal/511/Item-10-Best-
Friend-Work.aspx

Gartner: http://www.gartner.com/newsroom/id/2689817

Harvard Business Review: https://hbr.org/2015/04/what-great-managers-
do-to-engage-employees

CBS   News: http://www.cbsnews.com/news/why-success-is-all-
about-relationships/

The Pursuit of Happiness: http://www.pursuit-of-happiness.org/
science-of-happiness/communicating/

Acknowledgements

This book is proof of the power of meaningful connections and how goals are achieved through effective relationships! This started as an idea—a nutty idea—and would have remained in its shell without the tremendous support of so many talented, generous, and supportive people. I am grateful for all of these nuts.

A Nut-of-All-Trades

It was a summer afternoon and I was sitting al fresco, staring at my laptop, hoping the glass of wine I ordered would lead to inspiration to move me out of my stuck place in the writing process. I decided it was time to start working with an editor, so I Google searched local editors and found Debbie Johnson. I cold-called her, she answered, we set up a time to discuss my project, and after our first meeting the clouds cleared. She loved the project and got me moving again! Debbie is a nut-of-all-trades; business-marketing diva, best-selling author (Think Yourself Thin), filmmaker, producer, director, healthy chef, and editor. She was precisely the right partner to help me get "unstuck" and move through the writing, publishing, and marketing processes. She also connected me with many other wonderful nuts who contributed to this book; a special shout out to Jocelyn Parrish for her eyes and insights, Sue Jenkins for her ideas and expertise, and John Houlgate for his creativity and attention to detail!

A Truly Artistic Nut

Prior to class for coaching certification, I was chatting with a colleague when an enthusiastic woman with the most engaging smile walked into the room. She introduced herself, "Hi, I'm Lisa Fenton!" We became fast friends during the next few days. I told her about my book and that I was on the hunt for an illustrator, looking through several portfolios. After hearing a brief synopsis of the project, she asked if I'd be open to letting her draw a few quick illustrations to see if they might be a fit. She had artistic abilities that I envied during the drawing exercises in class, so of course I said, "Absolutely!" However, I had no idea in that moment that this corporate nut (specializing in Leadership Development at Target), who is also a wife and a busy mom, would be the person I had been wishing for to bring this book to life! Now I can't imagine working with anyone else. Lisa literally read my brain better than I could describe what I was thinking. I have been honored and grateful to collaborate on this project with such an amazing and talented nut!

Nutty Friends and Colleagues

The circumstances surrounding this book, start to finish, produced an assortment of nuts—willing to be cracked—who contributed to its completion in a number of ways. To all of my friends and colleagues who mentored me, provided honest feedback, promoted this mission, and believe in me, I am grateful to you all for your time, kindness, and support. There are a handful of nuts that I'd like to spotlight: Ruth (Ruthie) Godfrey and Jennie Antolak for being admirable women, awe-inspiring coaches, and running the best coaching institute: Learning Journeys, The International Center of Coaching. I deeply appreciate your support and cheerleading. Erica Vermeij, a dear friend who is another nut-of-all-trades: a wife, mother, businesswoman, chef/foodie, artist, and photography buff! Thank you for your support and the photo shoot! And Shelley Swartzel for believing in me, supporting my nutty plan, and pumping me up when I needed it.

I'd be remiss not to mention a few business nuts for whom I've been fortunate and privileged to work. They have shaped who I am and strive to be professionally: Mike Dowd was my first boss in Corporate America after I exited college. He set the example for how powerful meeting in person and being fully present is in building trust and effective relationships. Deb Syvertsen exemplified how to be a confident, credible, authentic leader, and how to effectively work with anyone in any situation. I have also always admired her ability to balance work with other priorities, honoring her values. Amador Lucero has an ability to inspire entire organizations from the front line to the back room, and throughout all levels of management. He is open, honest, and acts with integrity, which solidifies others' trust and confidence in his leadership.

Family of Nuts

At the heart of all that I do is my family. I happen to have the kindest, most wonderful husband/BFF on the planet, who is also my biggest supporter. He makes me laugh when I want to frown, and has taught me to chill-out when I get a little too nutty. We have beautiful daughters, on the inside and out. Our youngest was a miraculous and wonderful surprise. Her arrival provided the inspiration I needed to make the changes I had dreamt about! We also have two adorable dogs; it's a good thing they are cute, because their naughty behavior drives us nuts!

I am fortunate to have loving, successful, and somewhat nutty parents who have set the example for my most coveted values: trust, integrity, hard work, accountability, and fun! I have an amazing, uber-talented sister and an awesomely cool brother-law, who together have a beautiful little girl. We have a large extended family, and I treasure every one of the relationships. In full transparency, I'd say our family is a little on the nuttier side, by average standards. But hey, we're all nuts! And that's what makes life interesting. It's the nuts in our life—all parts of our life—and our relationships with them that helps shape who we are, where we go, and what we do.